Write DESIGN & WRECK

Draw, Paint, Rip and Ruin this Book

chartwell
books

Inspiring | Educating | Creating | Entertaining

Brimming with creative inspiration, how-to projects, and useful information to enrich your everyday life, quarto.com is a favorite destination for those pursuing their interests and passions.

Published in 2023 by Chartwell Books,
an imprint of The Quarto Group
142 West 36th Street, 4th Floor
New York, NY 10018 USA
T (212) 779-4972 F (212) 779-6058
www.Quarto.com

10 9 8 7 6 5 4 3 2 1

Chartwell titles are also available at discount for retail, wholesale, promotional, and bulk purchase. For details, contact the Special Sales Manager by email at special-sales@quarto.com or by mail at The Quarto Group, Attn: Special Sales Manager, 100 Cummings Center Suite 265D, Beverly, MA 01915, USA.

ISBN: 978-0-7858-4202-6

Publisher: Wendy Friedman
Senior Managing Editor: Meredith Mennitt
Senior Design Manager: Michael Caputo
Editor: Cathy Davis
Designer: Sue Boylan

Printed in China

Write DESIGN & WRECK

Draw, Paint, Rip, and Ruin this Book

chartwell
books

Introduction

Find inspiration and beauty around you and explore your creativity with this unconventional book. This book is designed to help you silence your inner critic to explore uninhibited creativity. Whether you consider yourself an artist or have little artistic experience, each prompt will guide you in harnessing your creativity and creating your own style.

Each prompt is a starting point. Approach the prompts with an open mind and make them your own. The writing prompts are designed to be introspective and thought-provoking. The destructive and artistic prompts are meant to help you think outside the box. This is the space for you to experiment with different art materials, get messy, and write whatever you want.

There are no rules on how to use this book. Work through it in order or randomly turn to a page whenever you feel like creating. Use it to spark new ideas or help break through a creative block. It's also a great way to relieve stress and unwind.

Let your imagination run wild and have fun!

MAKE A
PAPER AIRPLANE
USING
THIS PAGE.

CLOSE YOUR EYES...

+

DRAW AN ANIMAL

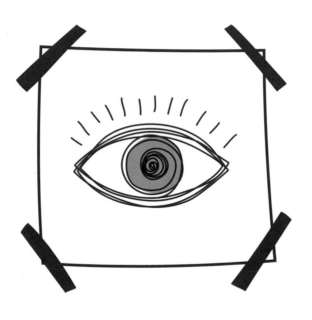

WHAT ARE YOUR
TOP 5 DREAMS
+ GOALS?

DESCRIBE YOUR iDEAL PLACE TO LiVE.

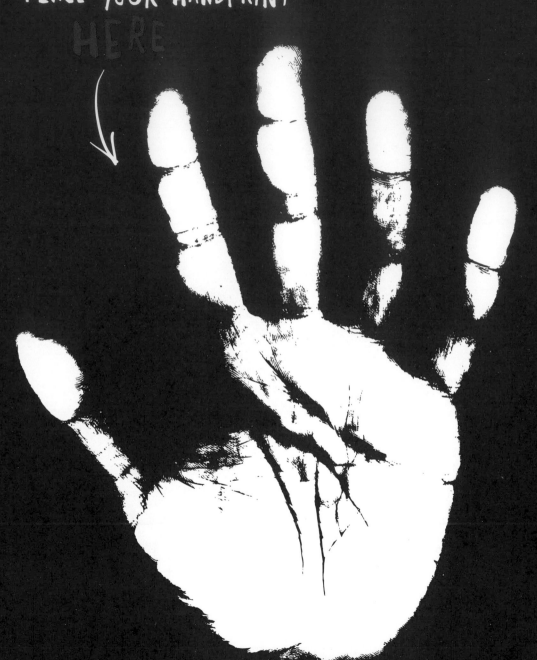

COVER THIS ENTIRE PAGE WITH STICKERS

PAINT YOUR
FAVORiTE PLACE
iN THE WORLD

DESCRIBE YOUR FAVORITE PLACE.

WHY IS IT YOUR FAVORITE AND HOW DO YOU FEEL WHEN YOU'RE THERE?

USE SCISSORS TO CUT
HOLES AND DESIGNS

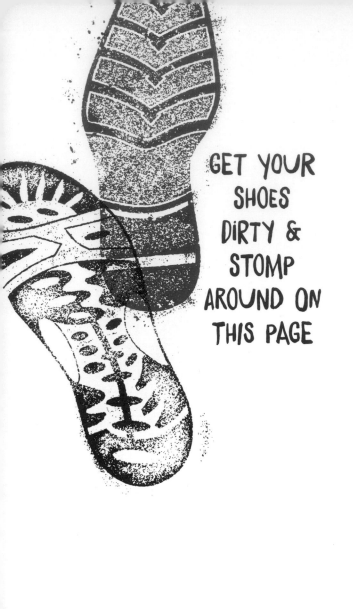

GET YOUR
SHOES
DIRTY &
STOMP
AROUND ON
THIS PAGE

DRAW A
SELF-PORTRAIT

HOW WOULD YOU DESCRIBE YOURSELF?

WHAT AREAS IN YOUR LIFE ARE YOU GROWING IN?

MAKE A COLLAGE
OUT OF SCRAPS OF
PAPER (RECEIPTS,
JUNK MAIL,
TICKET STUBS)

PRESS
LEAVES
& FLOWER
PETALS

WHAT ARE YOUR FAVORITE PLANTS AND FLOWERS? WHY DO YOU LIKE THEM?

HOW
DO YOU
FEEL
WHEN
YOU'RE
iN
NATURE?

DEAR

WRITE A LETTER TO SOMEONE AND THEN SOAK THIS PAGE IN A BOWL OF WATER

RUB YOUR FINGERS ON THE CIRCLE & THEN SMEAR THE PAGE ★

COLOR
IN THE
CIRCLE WITH
A PENCIL

MELT A PiECE OF CHOCOLATE HERE

DESIGN YOUR OWN
WRAPPING PAPER. USE
iT TO WRAP A GIFT
FOR SOMEONE.

WHAT TYPES
OF GIFTS
DO YOU LIKE
TO GIVE TO
FRIENDS AND
FAMILY?

WHAT ARE YOUR FAVORITE GIFTS TO RECEIVE?

USE YOUR NON-DOMINANT
HAND TO DRAW YOUR HOME

DESIGN AN
AMUSEMENT
PARK
ATTRACTION

WRITE DOWN ALL YOUR FRUSTRATIONS AND THEN RIP THIS PAGE INTO

TINY PIECES

LIST FIVE
THINGS YOU'RE
GRATEFUL
FOR.

1.

2.

3.

4.

5.

WRITE A HAIKU ABOUT YOUR DAY.

PRACTICE HAND-LETTERING

SPREAD A
MIXTURE OF GLUE
AND BAKING SODA
HERE

CREATE
YOUR OWN
SUPERHERO

WHO INSPIRES
YOU AND WHY?

DRAW OBJECTS FROM THE '60s

POKE HOLES
ALL OVER
THIS PAGE

DESIGN A FLOOR PLAN FOR YOUR DREAM HOME

DESCRIBE YOUR
CHILDHOOD HOME.

WHAT ARE
YOUR FAVORITE
CHILDHOOD
MEMORIES?

MAKE A
PAPER
SNOWFLAKE
USING THIS
PAGE

PRACTICE
DRAWING
FACES

RECIPE

NAME: _____

_____
_____
_____
_____
_____
_____
_____
_____
_____

RECIPE

NAME: _____

_____
_____
_____
_____
_____
_____
_____
_____
_____

WHICH FOOD
BRINGS BACK
MEMORIES
FOR YOU?

PIN
FABRIC
SAMPLES
HERE

MAKE
CONFETTI

DESIGN A NEW RESTAURANT

FREE WRITE
WITHOUT STOPPING
FOR 10
MINUTES.

NO EDITING!

WHAT THOUGHTS
AND EMOTIONS
CAME UP FOR
YOU WHILE
FREE WRITING?

CREATE A
TISSUE PAPER
MOSAIC

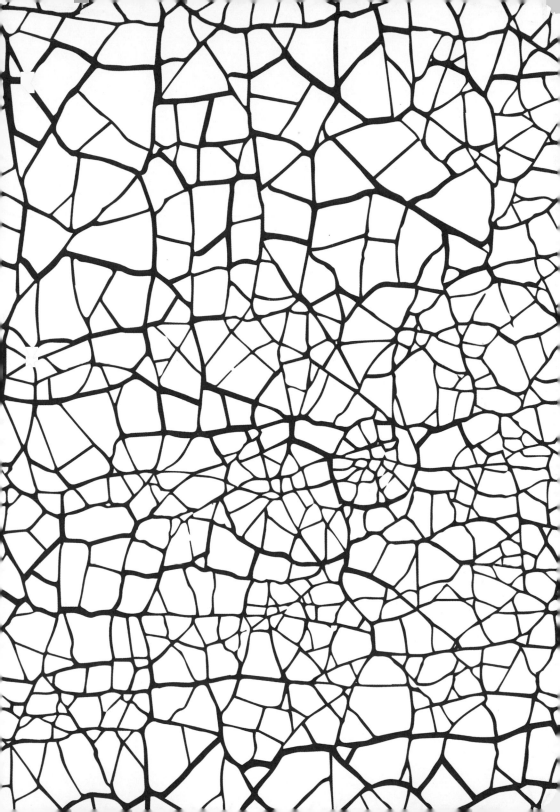

PLAN YOUR DREAM VACATION

LIST THE TOP FIVE PLACES YOU WANT TO VISIT.

WHAT DO YOU
ENJOY ABOUT
TRAVELING?
HOW DOES
TRAVELING
INSPIRE YOU?

SMASH
SOME
FOOD
CRUMBS
HERE

SKETCH TATTOO IDEAS

TAPE
SODA CAN
TABS
HERE

CREATE A PAPER CROWN

WHAT WERE YOUR FAVORITE
ACTIVITIES WHEN
YOU WERE A CHILD?

DO YOU STILL DO THEM TODAY? iF NOT, WHY?

RIBBON PAGE

DRAW
OBJECTS
FROM THE
'70s

RUB CHALK
ALL OVER
THIS PAGE

SKETCH
OUTFIT IDEAS

WHAT MAKES YOU
FEEL CONFIDENT?

JOT DOWN A
FEW POSITIVE
AFFIRMATIONS.

PAINT A FALL SCENE

RUB SOIL OR DIRT ON HERE

GLUE A PICTURE OF YOUR PET

WRITE ABOUT ANY
PETS YOU'VE HAD
THROUGHOUT YOUR
LIFE. DESCRIBE THEIR
PERSONALITIES AND
YOUR FAVORITE
MEMORIES WITH THEM.

CREATE A
PAINTING
WITH YOUR
THUMBPRINTS

DOODLE FLORALS AND BOTANICALS

TRACE RANDOM
HOUSEHOLD
OBJECTS (i.e.
TV REMOTE,
TOOTHBRUSH,
ETC.)

DESIGN A LOGO FOR A NEW COMPANY

IF YOU WERE TO START YOUR OWN BUSINESS, WHAT WOULD IT BE? DESCRIBE THE PROVIDED SERVICES OR PRODUCTS.

GLUE **CRAFT**
MATERIALS HERE
(YARN, BEADS, GEMSTONES, ETC)

POUR
OLIVE
OIL &
SPRINKLE
SPICES
HERE

CREATE A
LOOK FOR AN
AWARD SHOW

LIST YOUR TOP FIVE ACCOMPLISHMENTS.

1. _____
_____
_____
_____
_____

3. _____
_____
_____
_____

2. _____
_____
_____
_____

5. _____

4. _____
_____
_____

DO YOU STRUGGLE WITH CELEBRATING YOUR ACCOMPLISHMENTS OR SHARING YOUR CREATIVE TALENTS WITH OTHERS? WHY?

DESIGN A NEW PLANET

TRY A NEW
ART MEDIUM

USE
FOOD
COLORING
HERE

MAKE A PLAYLIST TO INSPIRE CREATIVITY

WHAT ARE SOME OF YOUR FAVORITE SONGS?

WRITE ABOUT SONGS OR MUSIC THAT AFFECT YOUR MOOD AND BRING YOU JOY.

CREATE A MIXED MEDIA COLLAGE

PAINT
WITH
NAIL
POLISH

WHAT IS YOUR CURRENT JOB? WHAT DO YOU LIKE AND DISLIKE ABOUT IT?

_____
_____
_____
_____
_____
_____
_____
_____
_____
_____
_____
_____
_____
_____
_____
_____
_____

DESCRIBE
YOUR DREAM
JOB

COLOR-
WiTH
CRAYONS

CREATE A COLOR PALETTE

DRAW
OBJECTS
FROM THE '80s

DESIGN A BOOK COVER

WRITE DOWN YOUR FAVORITE BOOK QUOTES.

"

"

WHAT WAS THE
LAST BOOK
YOU ENJOYED
READING? WHAT
DID YOU LIKE
ABOUT IT?

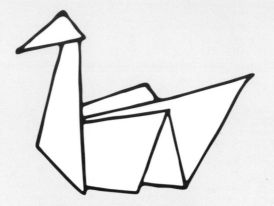

FOLD THIS PAGE
UNTIL IT'S TOO
SMALL TO FOLD

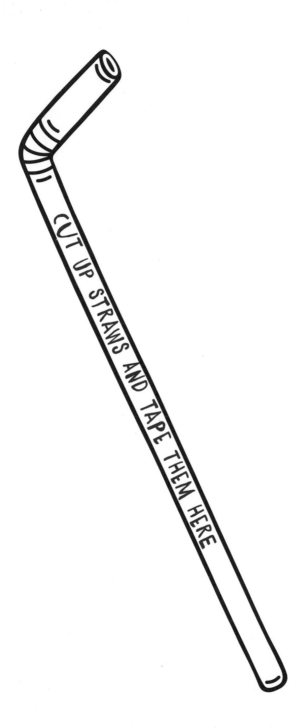

CUT UP STRAWS AND TAPE THEM HERE

DRAW A MAGICAL FOREST

IF YOU COULD HAVE
MAGICAL POWERS,
WHAT WOULD THEY BE?

WHAT WOULD
YOU DO
WiTH THOSE
POWERS?

CREATE A TERRARIUM

DRAW
OBJECTS
FROM
THE
'90s

SPRAY
WATER ON
THE
PLANTS

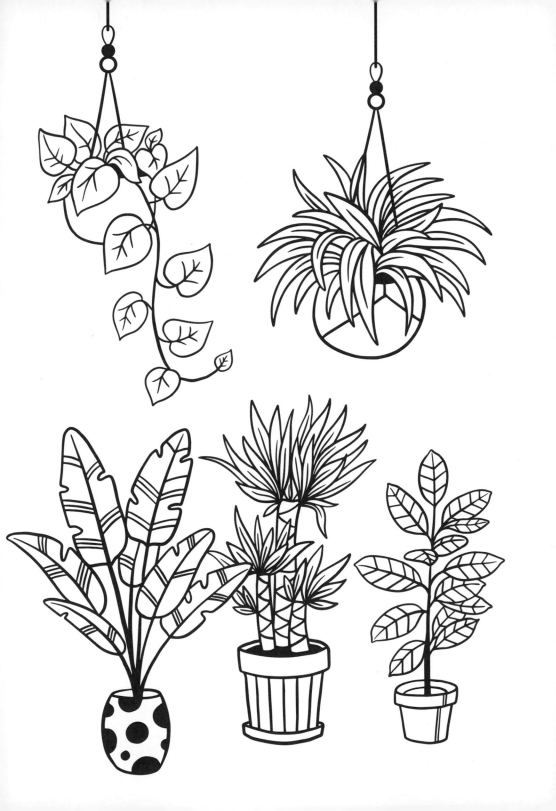

CREATE AN ABSTRACT PAINTING

DRAW AN
OBJECT
WITH
SENTIMENTAL
VALUE

WRITE ABOUT YOUR MOST LOVED POSSESSIONS AND WHY THEY'RE SPECIAL TO YOU.

USE ALL OF YOUR COLORED
PENCILS AND MARKERS HERE

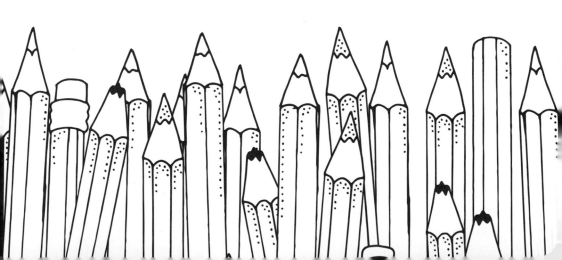

USE CONDIMENTS TO PAINT

ILLUSTRATE YOUR TO-DO LIST FOR THE WEEK

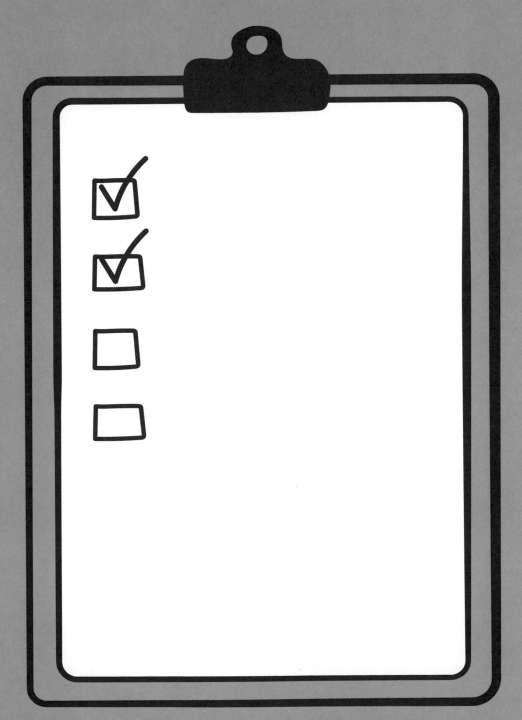

WHAT CAN YOU DO DAILY TO ADD MORE PEACE AND RELAXATION TO YOUR LIFE?

WHAT IS YOUR IDEAL WEEKEND?

RELOADING...

DRAW
A HOT AIR
BALLOON

TEAR UP THIS PAGE

THEN TAPE
THE PIECES BACK
TOGETHER

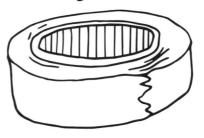

PAINT A SUNRISE

PAINT A SUNSET

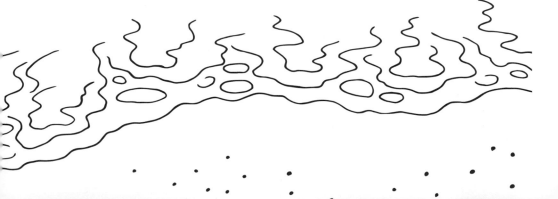

WHAT ARE YOUR MORNING AND EVENING ROUTINES?

HOW CAN YOU INCLUDE MORE FUN AND CREATIVITY INTO YOUR DAILY ROUTINES?

SPREAD JAM
ON THIS PAGE

Jam

PAINT AN
UNDERWATER
SCENE

LIST
YOUR
TOP
FIVE
FAVORITE
MOVIES.

1.

2.

3.

4.

5.

WHY DO YOU
LOVE THESE
MOVIES?
DESCRIBE HOW
THEY MAKE
YOU FEEL
WHEN YOU
WATCH THEM.

DRAW A
LANDSCAPE
USING ONLY
HIGHLIGHTERS

NOW MAKE IT IN YOUR OWN STYLE

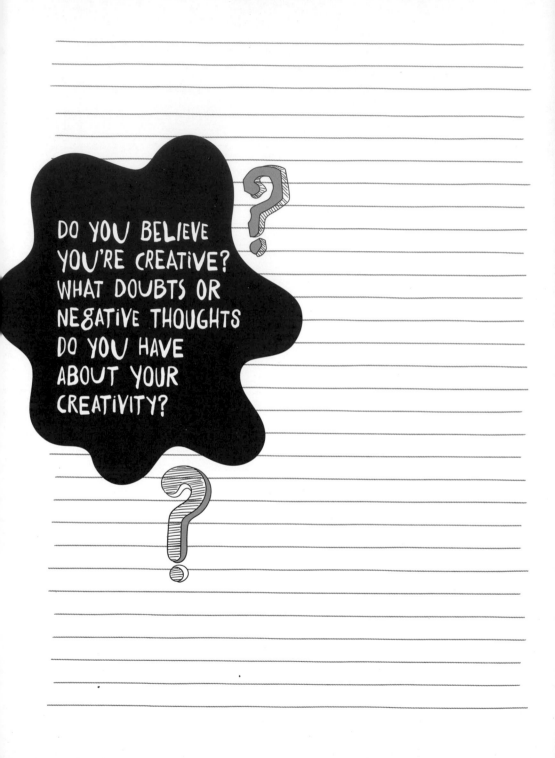

DO YOU BELIEVE YOU'RE CREATIVE? WHAT DOUBTS OR NEGATIVE THOUGHTS DO YOU HAVE ABOUT YOUR CREATIVITY?

RE-WRITE
YOUR NEGATIVE
THOUGHTS AS
POSITIVE ONES.

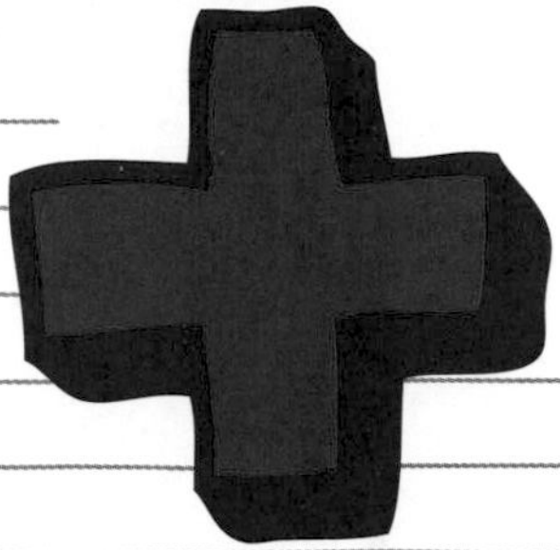

PAINT SOMETHING USING ONLY...

ONE COLOR

DESIGN A WREATH AND GLUE ON LEAVES, FLOWERS, ETC.

SCRIBBLE
PAGE

BRAINSTORM
NEW iDEAS

WHERE DO
YOU FIND
INSPIRATION?

WHAT DO YOU DO
WHEN YOU HAVE
A CREATIVE BLOCK?

MAKE A
COLLAGE
OUT OF
GRAINS
(RICE, OATS,
CEREAL, ETC.)

DRAW A MUSICAL INSTRUMENT

DESIGN A POSTAGE STAMP

WRITE SOMEONE A THANK YOU NOTE AND MAIL IT.

DEAR _____,

_____
_____
_____
_____
_____
_____
_____
_____
_____
_____
_____
_____
_____
_____
_____
_____
_____
_____
_____
_____
_____
_____

PAINT
SOME
ROCKS
AND STAMP
THEM HERE

CONNECT
THE
DOTS

PAINT A
WINTER
SCENE

WRITE ABOUT
YOUR FAVORITE
HOLIDAY
TRADITIONS.

WHAT DO YOU ENJOY THE MOST ABOUT THE HOLIDAYS?

DOODLE SPIRALS

DOODLE SPIRALS

DOODLE SPIRALS

DOODLE SPIRALS

DOODLE SPIRALS

DOODLE SPIRALS

TAPE YOUR
FAVORITE PHOTOS
OF FAMILY AND
FRIENDS HERE

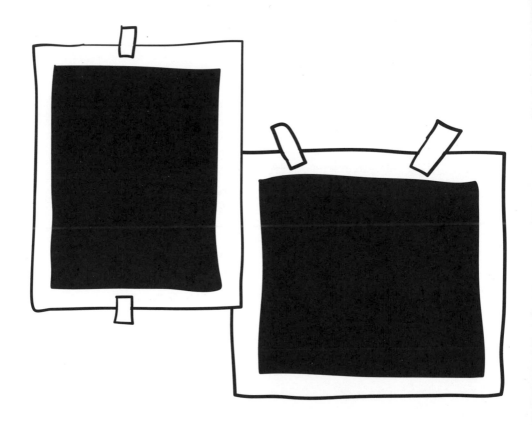

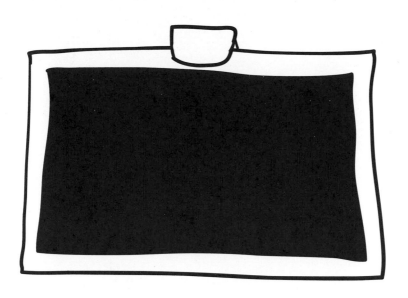

WRITE ABOUT THE MOST
IMPORTANT PEOPLE
IN YOUR LIFE. WHAT
DO YOU APPRECIATE THE
MOST ABOUT THEM?

HOW HAVE THEY
CHANGED YOU
OR YOUR LIFE?

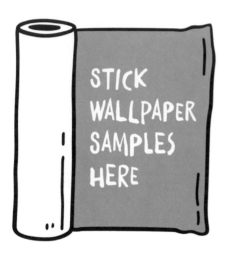

STICK WALLPAPER SAMPLES HERE

DRAW A GNOME

DESIGN A
BOOKMARK

PRACTICE DRAWING SOMETHING THAT'S DIFFICULT #%💀!

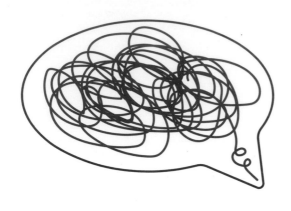

WHAT'S THE HARDEST THING YOU'VE EVER HAD TO DO?

_____
_____
_____
_____
_____
_____
_____
_____
_____
_____
_____
_____
_____
_____
_____
_____
_____

WHAT DID
YOU LEARN
FROM THAT
EXPERIENCE?

MAKE A PAPER BOW
USING THIS
PAGE

DESIGN WALL TILES

TAPE BUSINESS
CARDS HERE

PRACTICE CONTINOUS LINE DRAWING

GOLD STAR PAGE